Journal
Heart-Centered Wellness

1ST EDITION
BY THERESA A. W. VELENDZAS (AKA THERESAWV)

©Copyright Theresa A. Velendzas
Altraform, LLC 2021
www.Altraform.com

Heart-Centered Wellness Journal - 1st Edition
By Theresa A. W. Velendzas (aka TheresaWV)
ISBN: 979-8-9850072-1-3

Illustrations & Design ©Copyright 2021 by Deborah Zafiropoulos
Photography ©Copyright 2021 by Theresa Velendzas & Deborah Zafiropoulos

20 ____

January
S	M	T	W	T	F	S
☐	☐	☐	☐	☐	☐	☐
☐	☐	☐	☐	☐	☐	☐
☐	☐	☐	☐	☐	☐	☐
☐	☐	☐	☐	☐	☐	☐
☐	☐	☐	☐	☐	☐	☐
☐	☐	☐				

February
S	M	T	W	T	F	S
☐	☐	☐	☐	☐	☐	☐
☐	☐	☐	☐	☐	☐	☐
☐	☐	☐	☐	☐	☐	☐
☐	☐	☐	☐	☐	☐	☐
☐	☐	☐	☐	☐	☐	☐
☐						

March
S	M	T	W	T	F	S
☐	☐	☐	☐	☐	☐	☐
☐	☐	☐	☐	☐	☐	☐
☐	☐	☐	☐	☐	☐	☐
☐	☐	☐	☐	☐	☐	☐
☐	☐	☐	☐	☐	☐	☐

April
S	M	T	W	T	F	S
☐	☐	☐	☐	☐	☐	☐
☐	☐	☐	☐	☐	☐	☐
☐	☐	☐	☐	☐	☐	☐
☐	☐	☐	☐	☐	☐	☐
☐	☐	☐	☐	☐	☐	☐
☐	☐	☐				

May
S	M	T	W	T	F	S
☐	☐	☐	☐	☐	☐	☐
☐	☐	☐	☐	☐	☐	☐
☐	☐	☐	☐	☐	☐	☐
☐	☐	☐	☐	☐	☐	☐
☐	☐	☐	☐	☐	☐	☐
☐	☐	☐				

June
S	M	T	W	T	F	S
☐	☐	☐	☐	☐	☐	☐
☐	☐	☐	☐	☐	☐	☐
☐	☐	☐	☐	☐	☐	☐
☐	☐	☐	☐	☐	☐	☐
☐	☐	☐	☐	☐	☐	☐

July
S	M	T	W	T	F	S
☐	☐	☐	☐	☐	☐	☐
☐	☐	☐	☐	☐	☐	☐
☐	☐	☐	☐	☐	☐	☐
☐	☐	☐	☐	☐	☐	☐
☐	☐	☐	☐	☐	☐	☐
☐	☐	☐				

Agust
S	M	T	W	T	F	S
☐	☐	☐	☐	☐	☐	☐
☐	☐	☐	☐	☐	☐	☐
☐	☐	☐	☐	☐	☐	☐
☐	☐	☐	☐	☐	☐	☐
☐	☐	☐	☐	☐	☐	☐
☐	☐					

September
S	M	T	W	T	F	S
☐	☐	☐	☐	☐	☐	☐
☐	☐	☐	☐	☐	☐	☐
☐	☐	☐	☐	☐	☐	☐
☐	☐	☐	☐	☐	☐	☐
☐	☐	☐	☐	☐	☐	☐
☐	☐	☐				

October
S	M	T	W	T	F	S
☐	☐	☐	☐	☐	☐	☐
☐	☐	☐	☐	☐	☐	☐
☐	☐	☐	☐	☐	☐	☐
☐	☐	☐	☐	☐	☐	☐
☐	☐	☐	☐	☐	☐	☐
☐	☐	☐				

November
S	M	T	W	T	F	S
☐	☐	☐	☐	☐	☐	☐
☐	☐	☐	☐	☐	☐	☐
☐	☐	☐	☐	☐	☐	☐
☐	☐	☐	☐	☐	☐	☐
☐	☐	☐	☐	☐	☐	☐
☐	☐					

December
S	M	T	W	T	F	S
☐	☐	☐	☐	☐	☐	☐
☐	☐	☐	☐	☐	☐	☐
☐	☐	☐	☐	☐	☐	☐
☐	☐	☐	☐	☐	☐	☐
☐	☐	☐	☐	☐	☐	☐
☐	☐	☐				

Resources

Heart-Centered Wellness Journal

The Heart-Centered Wellness Journal is a customizable pathway to meeting your changing needs that is infused with tips and prompts to reflect on feelings, food, and exercise. This mind body journal contains two main parts: Resources for Nourishing Essentials, followed by a 15-Month Calendar to record your experiences. Personalize these to craft beloved self-care routines and integrate them into your life with ease. The resources section serves as a reference guide which includes a compilation of information at your fingertips, while the calendar section offers engaging prompts to record your experience along the way. Use colors, get creative, and enjoy the process. Get curious about your patterns and inner dialogue and adjust to your needs. This journal will nurture you to make your wellness and insight more intuitive so that you can infuse your life with sustainable health-building practices.

In order to make anything intuitive we need to pause and reflect on what is happening inside. This is why the IFS (Internal Family Systems) model discussed in the following pages plays an integral role here in that it invites curiosity around your experience. A departure from the "reprogramming approach" prevalent in wellness and self help, IFS offers a way to process and build sustainable lifelong habits. Insight into our inner chatter can bring awareness to underlying needs so we can better meet them which can in turn calm and strengthen our system. What would it be like to look forward to your healthy habits instead of constantly policing or enforcing them? What might it feel like to better understand your inner saboteur so that you can calm it in ways that do not derail you?

Another important component is Mindfulness. All mindfulness activities here fall under the umbrella of Heart-Centered Moments (HCM). These can range in length and entail brief pauses throughout the day. With no meditation expertise required, these HCMs facilitate check-ins to foster presence. If you are a meditator, you can integrate this practice and continue to keep track of your progress in the HCM sections provided.

Intake and movement are integral to self care regardless of your approach. Our bodies need food and movement to flourish and take us where we want to be both literally and beyond. The way we feel in our body invariably affects the way we show up and the decisions we make. We are more overweight than ever before and regardless of size, we seem preoccupied with weight loss. If weight loss is your goal I encourage you to find a research based way of eating that will fuel and restore your body. Adapting this to your life or household may entail cooking ahead or keeping some ingredients stored separately to offer choices for mixing and matching. Once you create a system, it can flow with ease to minimize reliance on overprocessed easy solutions. Already have a system? Use these pages to dive deeper so that your healthy way of eating becomes intuitive and sustainable.

Daily movement is both restorative and strengthening for all ability levels. Choose appealing activities to bring your heart rate up and build your endurance. Your body will love you for it and you will enjoy the effects of lower stress levels and boosted energy. Of course, every body, heart, and mind requires rest. Get recommended levels of sleep every day and engage in sleep hygiene activities to bring calm.

The following quick essential resources provide a core framework for creating your individualized path to wellness.

"The Heart Centered Path to Intuitive Wellness amplifies your self care for genuine, lasting success."

This self help journal is not a replacement for personal training, dietetic recommendations, clinical advice or therapy but may complement them with guidance. It is completely normal on a self help journey to seek more personalized support as needs arise.

Self Care

For the purposes of this work, "self care" is defined as nourishing your body, mind and spirit in ways where one does not adversely affect the other. Activities that fall under self care cannot be damaging to our system in other ways. Using this point of reference, if we find ourselves engaging with what we might intend as self care and find ourselves hurting ourselves in other areas, then it's time to get curious and reflect. Below is a table with ideas for self care. Use the open spaces to add your ideas as a first step to sprinkling them into your schedule.

Scheduling self care can be triggering -particularly around fitness, food, or anything that involves slowing down in today's "doing- centered" culture. Try to incorporate 30 minutes of movement a day in ways that feel right for you. Use the exercises in this journal to reflect on Use the exercises in this journal to reflect on what comes up for you. Invite curiosity into your practice.

Ideas to Embody Self Care

	My List /Ideas
Heart-Centered Moments	_____
Walking in Nature	_____
Exercise	_____
Creative Expression:	_____
(Singing, Dancing, Art, Writing, Music etc)	_____
Hobbies	_____
Connecting with a friend/loved one	_____
Pets	_____
Gardening	_____
Swimming, Floating, Showering	_____
Stretching	_____
Decorating / Decluttering	_____
Reading	_____
Travel	_____
Visiting a local attraction	_____
Gratitude Journaling	_____
Writing a letter to someone	_____
Charity work	_____
Cooking a fancy meal	_____
Take a class	_____
Do something you always wanted to	_____
Plan to Take a day off	_____

The Internal Family Systems (IFS) model by Richard Schwartz, Ph.D. offers a simple and elegant framework for psychological health that impacts the way we feel and as a result, how we show up in our world. An evidence based therapeutic modality, IFS helps navigate the inner dialogue we all experience. Each of us has a unique network of thought patterns, referred to as "parts" and also known as our inner constellation which exists around our inner essence, our "self". Parts include the persona we have for example at work, home, play, in relationship and even our inner saboteur. We can be highly efficient and effective in these roles that can also be at odds with each other. A desire or need to do one thing can easily contradict another. An optimistic part that starts a self-care program may be sabotaged by an ambitious part that considers self-care to be a luxury or worse, undeserved. This inner pull within us is known as a polarization that can hijack our best intentions. Parts can play several roles. Taking time to reflect and self care is a good way to facilitate connection with ourselves to experience our bodies from within.

At the heart of this internal system is our inner Self. We feel this very clearly when we are in the proverbial zone. What activities put you in the zone? When do you feel most creativity, calm, curiosity, connectedness, compassion, clarity, courage, or confidence? These 8 c-word qualities at varying levels comprise the quality of self known as self leadership. Parts find balance when they have enough of this Self energy. Sometimes it is hard to see Self, particularly if we have experienced trauma so please know this happens.

Parts develop in our lifetime through our experiences. They can generally be organized into one of three categories and still carry distinctive attributes like a person might. The 3 classifications of parts are: Managers, Firefighters, and Exiles and these all exist around our Self in our unique inner constellation. We all have them although their type and levels of expression vary. These categories serve as a framework to help us identify aspects of our inner constellation. Identifying the parts of our inner constellation at play can bring better self awareness so that we can address needs in better ways and change patterns that don't serve us.

Managers are the parts of us that we often admire for handling our day to day operations and projects. They help us stay organized, on task, and safe among other things. However sometimes they can also flood us with unpleasant emotions. They can show up as our inner critic for example, to help us avoid undesirable situations. Managers exist to help us show up in the best way possible and also to protect our system from threats.

Firefighters are the parts that react to a perceived threat or pain by taking extreme action that we may have difficulty stopping in the moment. Behaviors can be self-sabotaging or worse yet- destructive. Have you ever felt like you knew you were making a poor choice but still felt compelled to keep going? We see this in eating behaviors, relationships, and behaviors that harm our system. Firefighters are the parts of us reacting to a perceived threat to find immediate comfort in the moment even at a cost. Like the name indicates, the house fire may be put out but there will also be a mess to clean up. If this resonates for you, get curious about this part's intention for you. See what it is protecting and how you might be able to attend to that need in more healthful ways. This compassionate approach takes away the need to overpower ourselves or worse, feel weaker if we can't.

Exiles are the hurt parts of us guarded by Managers and/or Firefighters. This part feels the pain from experiences such as shame, rejection, challenges and traumatic situations. It carries this pain, almost as though it's lost in time. When activated we can feel flooded and overwhelmed with very strong emotions similar to those in a past event. Recognizing this in ourselves can allow us the space to get needed resources so that we can promote healing and change patterns that no longer serve.

Although a lot of this deeper work traditionally takes place in the therapy room, daily micro practices and a holistic mind body approach are key to redesigning sustainable transformation. Food, exercise, heart-centered moments to check in with your inner constellation, and parts-work, are all essential in designing your individualized self care plan. Use this journal alone or in combination with coaching or therapy. If you would like to dive deeper into IFS you can find independent providers with their listed credentials in the Internal Family Systems Institute's directory here: www.ifs-institute.com/practitioners

Your favorite access point(s) into self leadership energy will vary at any given time. The following worksheet, offers prompts to feel into any of these words as an access to Self. This is the energy we often refer to as being "in the zone". Use this worksheet to brainstorm ideas about how to tap into that energy source, and then add this to your self-care routine. Doing this can be helpful and may also activate some inner concerns. You can note them in your reflections and/ or the Drawing Parts section.

When checking in with or identifying parts, you may find yourself seeing these parts as subpersonalities. This process creates an inner sense of spaciousness that allows us to notice before we act. Checking in can help expand this spaciousness to allow curiosity, courage, compassion, calm, clarity, confidence, creativity, or a sense of connectedness to flow. If you would like to expand this spaciousness even further ask yourself: "How am I feeling toward this part?" The word "toward" addresses the heart instead of the head where we might default to in response to the word "about". If you are not feeling something along the lines of these C-words, chances are another part of you is taking over. Perhaps you are feeling judgement about a feeling coming up. As if that "judgement" were a person, ask if it can give you some space to get to know the what it is judging. If needed you can come back to it. Then ask yourself again how you are feeling toward the original part. Repeat until you might feel something along the lines of the C-words.

If you are feeling overwhelmed, take a break or ask feelings threatening to overwhelm you to give you space. This is different from suppressing or sending them away. You can ask parts to not overwhelm you while you extend curiosity to get to know them. Try it. Just politely ask, with the intention of getting back to them. You can get to know parts of yourself better through journaling, reflecting mindfully, and creating a deeper connection between your parts and your self with any of those c-word qualities.

For the purposes of this Journal, this brief IFS overview aims to facilitate compassionate self-care and enable a more intuitive process around understanding your needs, patterns, and inner dialogue. If a part of you takes over, get curious to see what it needs. I encourage you to practice speaking *for* your parts instead of *from* them. It's a great way to create space and gain clarity. For example, if I am feeling unmotivated to exercise I might speak for that part of me this way: Part of me doesn't feel like exercising at all and another part of me feels that if I fail to stick to my plan I will have failed... again. This example of an inner struggle shows a polarization. Most popular culture around fitness will promote pressure to perform so that one side wins. This nuance of speaking for our parts rather than from them helps create space and build relationship rather than suppress with more tension. Instead of forcing a tired manager part to push through, I may pause and notice that perhaps I have been already pushing too hard and actually need a rest. On the flip side, perhaps I'm tired from sitting at my computer for many hours and just know that if I can push through I will be glad I did. Getting curious about this can encourage self led, nourishing decisions. The "no pain - no gain" approach, though successful in bursts, typically yields short term, unsustainable results. It's tiring and temporary, like trying to hold a buoy underwater. Building habits and caring for yourself lovingly will yield more sustainable results than a drill sergeant's short-lived stress response.

Parts that sabotage our self care might be expressing fear or concern. It can be accompanied by many questions such as: What would happen if I changed a behavior? Why am I doing this? How does it serve my health and wellbeing? Is this a trailhead for me to do more personal development or maybe receive more support from a professional IFS coach or therapist? I encourage you to explore, celebrate and nurture yourself and your parts and their needs. It is a vital component towards weaving sustainable, health promoting behaviors into your everyday life. Befriending our inner chatter enables us to self care more compassionately.

Use the following worksheet to develop the theme of your self care plan. This worksheet can also act as a journal prompt in the reflection spaces offered throughout. Notice which C word pulls you more. Consider that an access point into your inner constellation and Self. Once you enter through one, say, creativity, you may feel increased self energy in other C areas as well. Allowing these feelings to flow will also build your intuition around healthy ways to implement self care micro practices in your life.

Self-Care Needs Assessment

Take a moment and read the words around the octagon. Circle ONE word that feels right in completing the sentence. Then write a short paragraph explaining how certain activities help you feel as though you are taking care of yourself in a way that strengthens your sense of self-leadership and nourishes you to be your best. Notice what feels right for you.

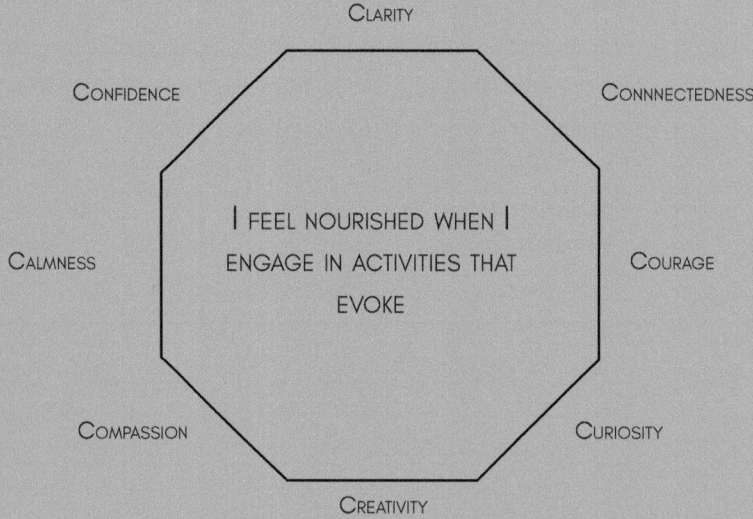

CLARITY

CONFIDENCE

CONNNECTEDNESS

CALMNESS

I FEEL NOURISHED WHEN I ENGAGE IN ACTIVITIES THAT EVOKE

COURAGE

COMPASSION

CURIOSITY

CREATIVITY

Activities I would like to integrate into my life (small/medium/large) include:

_____

_____

Daily / weekly/ monthly ideas to incorporate self care into micro and macro level:

_____

_____

Schedule these ideas into your day to nourish your Self.

Inspired by the Internal Family Systems Model. www.ifs-institute.com
Altraform, LLC. www.Altraform.com
All rights reserved.

Reflections

Self-Care Needs Assessment

Take a moment and read the words around the octagon. Circle ONE word that feels right in completing the sentence. Then write a short paragraph explaining how certain activities help you feel as though you are taking care of yourself in a way that strengthens your sense of self-leadership and nourishes you to be your best. Notice what feels right for you.

CLARITY

CONFIDENCE   CONNNECTEDNESS

CALMNESS   I FEEL NOURISHED WHEN I   COURAGE
                  ENGAGE IN ACTIVITIES THAT
                            EVOKE

COMPASSION   CURIOSITY

CREATIVITY

Activities I would like to integrate into my life (small/medium/large) include:

_____

_____

Daily / weekly/ monthly ideas to incorporate self care into micro and macro level:

_____

_____

Schedule these ideas into your day to nourish your Self.

Inspired by the Internal Family Systems Model. www.ifs-institute.com
Altraform, LLC. www.Altraform.com

Heart-Centered Moments (HCM)

Heart-Centered Moments (HCMs) are moments we take to reflect. These little pauses can be brief mindfulness moments sprinkled throughout your day and can take place anywhere from a morning stretch, to brushing your teeth, or meditating. For example, as you read these words, notice your breathing, your posture, and any tension you may be holding in your body. Perhaps you breathe more deeply as you bring your awareness to these. These moments can act as a grounding mechanism to bring awareness or self leadership qualities into your system. These moments foster presence and impact decisions about how we self care. If you feel challenged, start with curiosity and know that even that sometimes takes courage.

Incorporate HCMs as an act of pausing to focus on your breath and quickly give yourself time to ground. Though we all have expertise in breathing involuntarily, it takes a conscious decision to slow and control the breath. This very simple action impacts health by lowering heart rate, cortisol, and blood pressure. You do not have to be a mindfulness expert to practice this for the measurable benefits.

If you are incorporating meditation try extending curiosity to your inner chatter instead of suppressing or even allowing it to take over. This calm curiosity carries an energy of expansive self-compassion. Notice what it feels like to acknowledge your inner dialogue. Ask, what is this feeling trying to tell me about my needs? As you breathe into this exploration, you may ask this feeling or part to give you space and not overwhelm you. Often our manager parts might feel we are wasting time or failing and may distract us with more ideas such as "Am I doing this right?".

Take these Heart-Centered Moments throughout your day to check in with how it feels to connect with yourself with curiosity. Notice how many times a day you experience this awareness and circle a number 1-5 (or more) as prompted at the bottom of each day. Start a conversation about your unique interplay and synergy of your inner constellation and your path to heart-centered wellness. It changes for everyone and within that it ebbs and flows. Grounding moments enable body awareness and presence from within for precious feedback about our needs.

Tips for Heart-Centered Moments

- Sit by a window or outdoors and notice the colors.
- Tilt your head from side to side as you breathe and relax your jaw
- Place your right hand over your heart and your left hand on your belly while you breathe
- Try rubbing the tips of your fingers together so that you feel the ridges of your skin while taking some deep breaths.
- Try a 3-5 minute stretch breathing into each move
- Notice the sensation of water on your skin while washing your hands or in the shower.
- Find a quiet spot, soften your gaze, and breathe deeply.
- Hike in nature taking in the sights and sounds.
- Enjoy a cup of herbal tea, noticing the aroma and the sensations around drinking the beverage.
- Four Square Breathing:exhale for a count of 4, hold for 4, inhale for a count of 4 and pause for 4 before restarting. Repeat this for a few minutes to feel the effects on your body, heart, and mind.

Remain aware of your surroundings while practicing these and be safe.

Find your own ways to take pauses to breathe and notice your experience fully. This is a great time to reflect on what parts are coming up for you. Try incorporating a C-word (Calm, Curiosity, Courage, Creativity, Connectedness, Compassion, Clarity, Confidence) to parts of you working so hard to get you through your day. Each time will vary and that's ok.

Drawing Parts

Draw/ Sketch/ Write words to describe a "part" that you are getting to know. Remember to ask permission from the "part".

Drawing Parts can ignite curiosity around inner constellations. This can also be triggering so please proceed gently if you sense this may be the case for you. For one example, starting with your Self as the sun, draw circles to represent parts around it. Notice the varying distances between parts and self. You may want to even do a portrait of a Part to get to know it. Parts can look like words, objects, animals, or most commonly younger versions or ourselves. They have names and roles and at times don't get along with everyone in our inner system. Start where it feels comfortable.

Notice where you might feel a part in your body. Allow your inner dialogue to flow with questions starting with curiosity, permission, and compassion. We may not like all parts that come up and that is ok. We may really like others. If possible, notice what each one wants by speaking for them – a nuanced and significant difference with speaking from them. Expressing that "part of me feels X" instead of "I feel X" allows us the space to explore it in a more self-led way.

Ask a Part if it would be all right to get to know it. Compassionate parts exploration invites intention. Oftentimes this understanding evokes some form of positive feelings. For instance, part of me may feel defeated after a bad day and seek comfort that goes against my self care plan. Rather than a tough love approach or worse, shaming myself for failing again, perhaps this inner dialogue offers clarity and creativity to change a pattern or belief. What does reconciliation look like when you ask these questions? What type of self nourishment is missing? Curious exploration can open the doors to feelings of clarity, compassion, calm, confidence and more. This can lead to better choices.

Sometimes we may find that patterns may be attached to past painful experiences or trauma. If this is the case, please seek professional guidance from a qualified IFS therapist. If you find yourself flooded with emotions as you get to know parts, simply asking parts for space to get to know them slowly can be very powerful. Overwhelm is likely coming from another part, typically an "exile" reliving a past experience through a triggering situation. Acknowledging parts and offering self care can help build your relationship with your inner constellation. Similar to mindfulness, this process entails witnessing and acknowledging our thoughts. Journaling can help as well. The intention is to compassionately adapt self-care to your individual needs. If it works with you, it will also work for you.

A big reason why we are challenged to make healthy self care choices is because we have competing needs. What needs compete with your self care? Get to know them, nourish them and you will be on your way to sustainable growth. Away from punitive weight loss culture, you will find yourself better able to see and select resources instead of impossible challenges.

Use the following blank pages to draw a part or your inner constellation. Feel free to use bubbles or words. No artistic expertise required.

Drawing Parts

Draw/ Sketch/ Write words to describe a "part" that you are getting to know. Remember to ask permission from the "part".

My invitation to you is to explore a way of eating and movement that is doable where you are in this moment. Simply speaking, nourishing your body involves movement, a balanced whole foods diet, sleep hygiene, and stress self care which can include anything from breathing, to organization, and to preferred spiritual practices. Given we are all differently able and with differing needs, it is important that we tune into our own abilities without judgement. It is easy to lose sight of this and compare ourselves to others who we may perceive as being farther along- particularly in the world of fitness and weight loss but also in life. Self care and self nourishing will propel you toward the things that matter to you.

Movement

As you get started, evaluate your daily activity. Many of us do not get enough movement, time outdoors, or time in nature. Does counting steps motivate you? Perhaps a bike ride or dancing sounds appealing. Look for ways to experience your body in motion. What does your body feel like at the start, midpoint and end of physical activity? What does stretching feel like at different times of the day?

Alignment is an essential element in preventing movement injury and strengthening our foundation. It also helps us connect with our body and inner constellation. Notice feelings that come with changing posture or with movement. Where do you feel stress in your body? What happens when you loosen your jaw, roll your shoulders, step your feet on different surfaces such as a floor, grass or sand?

Stretching routines that comfortably challenge ability, help to restore posture and fluidity in movement. Muscle synergy becomes affected when we hold tension, a position for prolonged periods of time, or when we engage in repetitive movements. When one set of muscles is affected, their ability to contribute to movement becomes impaired and this leads to injury. Create mini stretching habits morning and evening. These can double

up as Heart-Centered Moments while restoring alignment and facilitating muscle recovery. Good posture means your muscles are working collaboratively, like a good team with all players showing up and doing their job. This prevents injuries and also facilitates exercise recovery.

Find an easy stretching sequence that feels good to your body and follow your movement with breathing intentionally. For example, try a child's pose with variations where you may lean from side to side. Try taking a few deep breaths in this pose and on the exhale walk your arms to one side. Stay for a few breaths and notice one side of your chest expand more. Repeat on the other side for a few breaths. Add variations with toes tucked under or wisened knees and notice the stretch in your feet and legs. Visualize, feel, and breathe into it. This 5 minute informal routine is a great way to start your day and step into your posture.

You do not have to be naturally flexible. In fact, stretching increases flexibility. You can find stretches

to do in bed, on your floor, seated or standing. It has many therapeutic benefits for people of all levels and abilities so find a modality you enjoy, whether live, virtual or informally on your own, and stretch safely. If you are experiencing muscle tightness, explore foam rolling resources and add them to your daily movement routine. It's easy, portable, and effective for loosening tension.

You also do not have to be an exercise fanatic to make a difference in your health. Add pockets of movement into your daily routine. A 25-minute daily brisk walk offers many benefits including stress reduction, a boost for your immune system, and natural weight regulation. Take a walk in your neighborhood or a local park. This can also serve as a heart-centered moment to check in.

A few considerations on walking posture. A quick tip is to tuck in your lower belly gently to engage your core while breathing comfortably and landing your step heel to toe gently. This can be applied to jogging also. Walking and running are valuable inexpensive ways to get exercise without fancy equipment anywhere you can carve out the time. Get comfortable shoes (always size up if running) and wear clothing that helps you exercise. Proper shoes are essential for supporting good body mechanics. If you are getting back into fitness, give yourself time and grace. Muscles have a wonderful way of remembering but also need time to adapt. Intensity can and does vary.

Running, for example, can fluctuate in intensity from a jog to a sprint and drills. Do what feels right for your body and try to keep challenging yourself comfortably by changing it up. If you have movement impairments, incorporate personalized corrective exercises. Movement is restorative.

Add a few days of strength training into your weekly plan through your favorite forms of exercise for success in helping your body perform optimally. Strength training can involve weights or your own body weight. It can even be done as part of a 10 minute break. If you are exercising at home, you may want to create a fun space simply with bands, a yoga ball, pull-up bar, dumbbells, a chair, and a mat. Use a full length mirror to check your posture and improve body awareness. You do not need fancy equipment to get the job done playfully. Having this as a main or even a backup to a gym membership will provide options that create distance from activating "all or nothing" thinking and closer to the "something every day" approach. Traveling to a gym daily may not be desirable or sustainable for you. While training for sport or competition can be fun, it is not necessary for wellness. Let the idea of fitness be flexible and organic to your needs. The cumulative effects of mini bursts of exercise count. Training for a goal counts. Walking daily counts. Modifying exercises to your ability counts. Find what works for you.

At night you may enjoy a nice spinal twist to release lower back tension. Laying flat with legs extended, bring in one knee for a brief hug, then bring it mid way back down and over to the opposite side of your body where it falls comfortably, for a few deep breaths. Notice the stretch expand as you hold. Repeat on the opposite side. Find the stretch that helps you wake up or relax before bed and make it part of your practice. Remember to breathe into stretches and slow down. The magic is in the hold. A 20-second hold in a position can loosen tension. Repeat that stretch after a brief break and feel yourself stretch more deeply. Listen to your body always.

You will likely cycle through different activities as you experiment. Try to stick with something for a month or a season to build habits and use your workbook to note how you feel. You might be surprised at how new favorites emerge and by the nuances you feel on different days. As you build endurance your heart health, posture, and muscle tone will improve to set off a series of other health benefits.

Allow for recovery days in between heavy exercise days. Too often we burn out by pushing too hard. Recovery can mean a day off, stretching, walking. A good schedule incorporates all of these consistently so use the calendar to track your activity. Start where you are and know that even trainers modify. Listening to our body really matters.

Flexibility is great but try not to let it undermine the value of a schedule. If you require more flexibility, try and create a few scenarios to pick from to help you build flow. Having a schedule and a buddy or an accountability partner significantly increases motivation and feelings of success. Consider joining one of our community groups to connect with others on their journey.

Below is a one week program you can repeat for a 6 week cycle and see and feel physical changes. Use the titles as keywords to search for free workouts you can save so that you can design your own schedule alone or in combination with classes, at your fitness level. Make sure the person you follow offers safety guidelines and has professional training. Use a mirror to spot yourself and be safe.

Proposed 8-Week Fitness Template

Monday	Tuesday	Wednesday	Thursday	Friday	Saturday	Sunday
Cardio or Legs, Glutes	Full body	Chest & Back	Core with Legs or Glutes	Back & Biceps	Shoulders & Triceps or Cardio	Restorative Stretching

Some tips on how to use this; on Cardio day you may choose to dance, full body day can be a barre class, and you may add restorative yoga for recovery days. Yoga is versatile in that it can also build strength. Consider engaging in activities seasonally for variety and for more of a heart-centered connection. Swimming, cycling, running, dancing, yoga, pilates, boot camp, climbing, rowing and sports are all great options that build endurance, muscle, and connect you intimately with your heart, mind and body. Feel yourself take action in different ways and give yourself grace for the fatigue everyone experiences. It's normal for your energy levels to vary. If you are already into the fitness portion, it may be time to change things up by adding in flexibility or agility training. You may add a specific goal such as improving speed or a long lost dream of doing a handstand. Be safe and enjoy being present in your body.

Fitness Ideas

Below are some ideas to help you plan and integrate movement into everyday living. Check ideas you like:

_____ Simple Stretches

_____ Steps

_____ Daily Brisk Walk

_____ Jogging

_____ Virtual Fitness

_____ Gym

_____ Home gym / equipment

_____ Sport _____

_____ Body/Weight Training
(Dumbbells, Bootcamp, Crossfit)

_____ Flexibility
(Yoga, Corrective Exercise, Pilates)

_____ Swimming

_____ Dance
(Choose pleasant music that suits your mood)

_____ Cycling

_____ Martial Arts

_____ Brief Challenges
(ie 7,21,30 days of squats)

_____ Hiking

_____ Climbing

_____ Sports Conditioning (Agility, Speed, Plyometrics)

Whole Foods Diet

Beyond nourishment and culture, each person's relationship with food is unique. Our way of eating has increasingly become more centered around highly processed, calorie dense convenience foods. The obesity epidemic continues to worsen despite an abundance of information about what to do and not do. What are we doing wrong? Perhaps we are feeding many needs in limited ways.

Find a way of eating that works for you. The whole foods list provided is for meal inspiration whether you are shopping, looking for snack ideas, or thinking about ingredients as key words for recipe / meal searches. Go for balance and lots of colorful vegetables. Explore reducing processed foods, limiting sugars, and adding a lot of nutrient dense, high fiber plants such as spinach, cabbage, broccoli and kale along with other favorite vegetables so that you pack more nutrition into your every meal. Fresh fruits, seeds and nuts are also fantastic energy dense sources. Be mindful to include your protein (veggies have protein too!) and healthy fats. Canada's updated food guidelines encourage a mostly plant based diet. You do not have to adhere fully to enjoy a lot of benefits. Simply cutting out processed meats and sticking with lean healthy cuts in moderation can have an impact on your wellbeing. The idea here is to be plant based instead of meat, wheat, and refined sugar based.

Cruciferous vegetables like kale, cauliflower and cabbage are commonly referenced for their immunity boosting properties. Other immunity boosting foods are berries, pomegranate, seeds, legumes, mushrooms, garlic and onions. Filling half your plate with nutrient dense vegetables every time will increase your nutrition value, boost immunity and help you reduce calories while helping you feel full. Include healthy fats like avocado and nuts and keep foods in suggested daily intake portions to avoid "too much of a good thing". Probiotics in the form of yogurt, kefir, or supplementation can help boost overall gut health. Explore options that work for you.

Pick what works for your palate and incorporate it into your meal prepping while basing all of it on veggies as much as possible. Across most eating plans many veggies especially steamed or raw are allowed in unlimited portions. There is no need to be hungry to manage your weight. Personalize and explore flavors. Focus on food varieties and portions rather than calorie counting. Avoid hunger as it eventually leads to problems.

Limiting artificial sweeteners can be hard at first. It gets better. Eliminate soda - even zero calorie soda and any calorie packed beverages as they can slow down the body's natural return to balanced weight. Ensuring daily water intake at around half your weight in ounces aids in digestion and overall functioning. Follow thirst prompts. Add water when you are sweating. If you don't like water plain, try infusing it with some lemon, fruit, or herbs for flavor and added health benefits. See some of my favorite ideas in the box below and don't be afraid to get creative with your own.

Cold Herbal Infusion Waters

Fill a pitcher with water and add herbs or fruit letting it sit for 12-24 hours to infuse with flavor. You can also make ice cubes for an easy addition to your water bottle on the go.

1. Mint: peppermint, spearmint, lemon balm, chocolate mint
2. Lemon, orange, lime rind.
3. Basil & Watermelon
4. Ginger
5. Raspberries / Strawberries / Blueberries
6. Floral: Jasmin, Rose Petals, Orange & Lemon Blossoms, Lavender, Lilac

Teas

Get a tea ball to make your own. Here are some yummy destressing ideas. Consider adding a piece of fresh ginger or apple for added flavor.

1. Chamomile
2. Mint
3. Rosehip
4. Passionflower Tea
5. Green Tea (has caffeine)

A note on meal prepping. Don't let the term conjure up images of cooking for hours on end. Consider grocery delivery or a healthy meal prep service instead of eating out. Make whole foods readily available in your fridge for snacking or easy access and assembly. Plan to incorporate 1-2 nutrient dense vegetables in every meal so shop in the correct amounts. Adding more veggies is a good way to transition if all of this sounds overwhelming. Make extra food for easy warm-ups, and plan a day or two ahead. These bite-sized changes can easily replace less healthy habits. Try to be consistent with the timing of meals and avoid eating late at night.

Talk to your doctor, dietician or related practitioner about your specific nutrition needs. Get regular checkups with medical professionals to assess your health needs. Get help if you have concerns around supplementation, digestion, bloating or weight loss struggle. You can take notes on your intake in the workbook to help you track your experience with your way of eating. Noting foods also helps create a more intuitive process and also helps you track your changing tastes as a result of eating more whole foods. Celebrate, restart, and notice with curiosity so you can adapt. Food journaling might be helpful to cycle through periodically.

Consider adding smoothies or juicing fruits and veggies to add nutrition but be careful to keep fruit servings appropriate to avoid adding a sugar bolus in one serving and driving up your blood sugar. Of special note on the difference between smoothies and juicing: Smoothies use a blender and keep the fiber in the beverage. This keeps you feeling fuller longer especially if you add a serving of protein or a healthy fat. It's a wonderful small meal or recovery snack after a tough workout. Juicing involves extracting only the juice and discarding the pulp which makes nutrient absorption more restful for your digestive tract. Juicing offers a delicious, easy to absorb, nutrition boost.

Whether you choose a style of eating such frequent small meals or intermittent fasting, go for consistency so that you can experience the effects (as long as it is medically approved for you). Both are backed by science which doesn't always agree. Choose a plan that you can envision meeting your needs and design a way to commit to it for a few days. If you find it desirable, you can tweak things so you can extend to a week, then a month or more. It's ok to change, but give it time also. Practice can deepen your sense of connectedness to the energy you receive from food and as a result strengthen your intuitive process.

Follow hunger cues for insight as to what might need adjusting. If you are on an eating plan that solely relies on hunger cues, try to attend to them in ways that don't leave you feeling guilty or needing to compensate. Refined sugar is a very hard, universally necessary one to cut back on that most people struggle with. You are not alone. Streamline your food intake to create habits, flow, and comfort.

Get curious about your unique relationship with food, your triggers, and how you feel as you take healthful action towards your overall wellness while fueling your system. Tracking this helps build clarity, consistency, and confidence.

Smoothie
In a Blender
$\frac{1}{2}$ cup flavored vegan milk (vanilla flax)
$\frac{1}{3}$ cup non dairy kefir
2 cups fresh or frozen spinach
1 cup frozen strawberries
$\frac{1}{2}$ frozen banana (optional)
1 tbsp MCT oil or avocado
Ice and water for preferred consistency

Juice
4-7 large kale leaves
1-2 large carrots
1 apple
1 knob of ginger (optional)

Foods for Inspiration

This list is a quick reference for nutrient-dense foods and is not all-inclusive. Whenever possible choose organic.

Legumes

Black-Eyed Peas	Edamame	Lima Beans	Red Kidney Beans
Chickpeas	Giant White Beans	Pigeon Peas	Split Peas
	Lentils	Pinto Beans	White Beans

Vegetables

Arugula	Cabbage	Garlic	Radishes
Asparagus	Carrots	Kale	Romaine
Beets	Celery	Micro Greens	Spinach
Bok Choy	Collard Greens	Mushrooms	String Beans
Boston Lettuce	Cucumber	Mustard Greens	Tomatoes
Broccoli,	Dandelion	Onion	Watercress
	Fresh & Dried Herbs,	Peppers	

Fruit

Apples	Grapes	Pear	Strawberries
Pears	Grapefruit	Pineapple	Tangerines
Banana	Kiwis	Plum	
Blueberries, Blackberries	Melon	Pomegranate	
	Orange	Raspberries	

Proteins

Cottage Cheese	Fish	Lamb	Seafood
Eggs	Grass Fed Beef	Poultry	Tofu
	Greek Yogurt	Pork	Tempeh

Carbohydrates

Amaranth	Millet
Barley	Oatmeal
Brown Rice	Pasta, GF Pasta
Cassava	Quinoa
Cereal	Sweet Potato, Potato
Crackers	Tortilla
Corn	Whole Grain & GF Bread
Quinoa	White Rice

Healthy Fats

Avocado	Pistachios
Almonds	Pumpkin Seeds
Cashews	Sesame
Coconut & Coconut Milk	Walnuts
Feta Cheese (Goat / Lamb)	Oils & Butters
Flax & Flax Milk	Coconut Oil, Extra Virgin
Hummus	Flaxseed Oil
Olives	Grass Fed Butter
Parmesan	MCT Oil
Peanuts	Olive Oil Extra Virgin
Pecans	Nut Butters
	Seed Butters

Sleep Hygiene

Sleep is often overlooked yet a significant percentage of the world's population reports not getting enough sleep. If you are feeling tired, you are not alone. Imagine how different our choices are when we are well rested. Sleep ties into our ability to manage stress which affects hormones, immunity, resilience, and overall health. It affects our food and movement, choices, as well as our inner (and sometimes outer) dialogue and performance.

Set a time to turn off electronics to rest from blue light for deeper sleep. You can set a bedtime reminder on a device to help keep you consistent. Create a calming bedtime routine. Let sleep become a favorite easy workout. Your digestion and metabolism will improve as will your skin, brain functioning and overall feeling of wellness. You may even find parts of yourself feeling much less burdened by your responsibilities and other parts stronger and more capable. Sleep is time well spent.

Self-care, fitness, food, maintaining a healthy weight, and our inner constellation are all interrelated and affect us all differently depending on our circumstances. It is completely normal to experience changes because life is ever changing. Yet, for some reason when we are not feeling our best, we tend to worsen the feeling by comparing ourselves to someone else's best. This can lead to feelings of frustration even before we even try to get back onto a wellness plan. It can also lead to restrictive and punitive approaches to self care. Strive for balance, listen to your feelings with caring curiosity and practice holistic self care through foundational support systems like regular checkups, healthy eating, movement, sleep and heart-centered moments to connect and reflect. It's impossible to keep a consistent schedule indefinitely. A more authentic, self led connection to your needs will empower more healthy restorative responses. Notice how this different way of self nurturing blossoms throughout your day and intuitively guides your self care. You are the only one who knows what your body feels like from the inside. Taking moments to notice and connect will guide your decision making in new ways so you can thrive. Visit www.altraform.com for updates, bonus materials, and a brief questionnaire. I would love to hear about your journey in the questionnaire or via email at theresa@altraform.com May your path to heart-centered wellness imbue your life with ripples of health and self leadership. Be well.

Let's Begin

Write or Draw your starting point today.

Workbook Key

PARTS WORK: What kind of energy did you feel today? Did you get to know a part? Where is it in your body? Does this part have a name?

MOVEMENT: Exercise type, Steps, Stretches, How did movement feel in your body?

FOOD AND WATER: How did it feel to nourish yourSelf? What kinds of foods did you eat? Any difficulties to explore any further?

HEART CENTERED MOMENTS: 1 2 3 4 5 Number of times you checked into your Self/ body?

What makes your creativity flow?

HEART CENTERED MOMENT PRACTICE

Month

S	M	T	W	T	F	S
☐	☐	☐	☐	☐	☐	☐
☐	☐	☐	☐	☐	☐	☐
☐	☐	☐	☐	☐	☐	☐
☐	☐	☐	☐	☐	☐	☐
☐	☐	☐	☐	☐	☐	☐
☐	☐	☐				

Weekly Intention and Notes

SUNDAY	MONDAY	TUESDAY	WEDNESDAY

Parts Work

Movement

Food & Water

1 2 3 4 5	1 2 3 4 5	1 2 3 4 5	1 2 3 4 5

SELF CARE THEME Some words that describe your Self care focus this week.

MONTH_____

THURSDAY	FRIDAY	SATURDAY	WEEK-END REFLECTION PARTS WORK, NOTES GRATITUDE, HIGHLIGHTS

_____ _____ _____

Parts Work

_____
_____
_____
_____
_____
_____

Movement

_____
_____
_____
_____
_____

Food & Water

_____
_____
_____
_____
_____

1 2 3 4 5   1 2 3 4 5   1 2 3 4 5

Extra Notes and Observations

Weekly Intention and Notes

SUNDAY	MONDAY	TUESDAY	WEDNESDAY

Parts Work

_____

Movement

Food & Water

1 2 3 4 5   1 2 3 4 5   1 2 3 4 5   1 2 3 4 5

SELF CARE THEME Some words that describe your Self care focus this week.

_____
_____
_____
_____
_____

MONTH _____

| THURSDAY | FRIDAY | SATURDAY | |

Parts Work

_____
_____
_____
_____
_____
_____
_____

Movement

_____
_____
_____
_____
_____

Food & Water

_____
_____
_____
_____
_____
_____
_____

1 2 3 4 5   1 2 3 4 5   1 2 3 4 5

_____
_____
_____
_____
_____
_____

Extra Notes and Observations

_____
_____
_____
_____
_____
_____
_____
_____
_____
_____
_____
_____
_____
_____
_____
_____
_____
_____
_____
_____
_____
_____
_____
_____

Weekly Intention and Notes

SUNDAY	MONDAY	TUESDAY	WEDNESDAY

Parts Work

Movement

Food & Water

1 2 3 4 5   1 2 3 4 5   1 2 3 4 5   1 2 3 4 5

SELF CARE THEME Some words that describe your Self care focus this week.

MONTH

THURSDAY _____

FRIDAY _____

SATURDAY _____

Parts Work

Movement

Food & Water

1 2 3 4 5   1 2 3 4 5   1 2 3 4 5

Extra Notes and Observations

Weekly Intention and Notes

SUNDAY	MONDAY	TUESDAY	WEDNESDAY

Parts Work

Movement

Food & Water

| 1 2 3 4 5 | 1 2 3 4 5 | 1 2 3 4 5 | 1 2 3 4 5 |

SELF CARE THEME Some words that describe your Self care focus this week.

M<small>ONTH</small>_____

T<small>HURSDAY</small>   **F<small>RIDAY</small>**   **S<small>ATURDAY</small>**

_____   _____   _____

Parts Work

Movement

Food & Water

1 2 3 4 5   1 2 3 4 5   1 2 3 4 5

Extra Notes and Observations

Weekly Intention and Notes

SUNDAY	MONDAY	TUESDAY	WEDNESDAY

Parts Work

Movement

Food & Water

1 2 3 4 5   1 2 3 4 5   1 2 3 4 5   1 2 3 4 5

SELF CARE THEME Some words that describe your Self care focus this week.

Month_____

THURSDAY	FRIDAY	SATURDAY

_____ _____ _____

Parts Work

Movement

Food & Water

Extra Notes and Observations

1 2 3 4 5   1 2 3 4 5   1 2 3 4 5

Heart Centered Moments

What were your heart-centered moments like?
What makes you feel more present?

GLOWS, GROWS AND HIGHLIGHTS

In autumn trees show us how lovely
it is to let the dead things go.

ADAGE

S	M	T	W	T	F	S

Weekly Intention and Notes

	SUNDAY	MONDAY	TUESDAY	WEDNESDAY

Parts Work

Movement

Food & Water

1 2 3 4 5	1 2 3 4 5	1 2 3 4 5	1 2 3 4 5

SELF CARE THEME Some words that describe your Self care focus this week.

MONTH

THURSDAY	FRIDAY	SATURDAY

Parts Work

Movement

Food & Water

1 2 3 4 5   1 2 3 4 5   1 2 3 4 5

Extra Notes and Observations

Weekly Intention and Notes

SUNDAY	MONDAY	TUESDAY	WEDNESDAY

Parts Work

Movement

Food & Water

| 1 2 3 4 5 | 1 2 3 4 5 | 1 2 3 4 5 | 1 2 3 4 5 |

SELF CARE THEME Some words that describe your Self care focus this week.

Month_____

THURSDAY	**FRIDAY**	**SATURDAY**

_____ _____ _____ _____ _____ _____

Parts Work

Movement

Food & Water

1 2 3 4 5   1 2 3 4 5   1 2 3 4 5

Weekly Intention and Notes

SUNDAY	MONDAY	TUESDAY	WEDNESDAY

Parts Work

Movement

Food & Water

| 1 2 3 4 5 | 1 2 3 4 5 | 1 2 3 4 5 | 1 2 3 4 5 |

SELF CARE THEME Some words that describe your Self care focus this week.

MONTH_____

| THURSDAY ____ | FRIDAY ____ | SATURDAY ____ | |

WEEK-END REFLECTION PARTS WORK, NOTES GRATITUDE, HIGHLIGHTS

Extra Notes and Observations

Parts Work

Movement

Food & Water

1 2 3 4 5   1 2 3 4 5   1 2 3 4 5

Weekly Intention and Notes

SUNDAY	MONDAY	TUESDAY	WEDNESDAY

Parts Work

Movement

Food & Water

| 1 2 3 4 5 | 1 2 3 4 5 | 1 2 3 4 5 | 1 2 3 4 5 |

SELF CARE THEME Some words that describe your Self care focus this week.

MONTH_____

THURSDAY ____	FRIDAY ____	SATURDAY ____	WEEK-END REFLECTION PARTS WORK, NOTES GRATITUDE, HIGHLIGHTS

Parts Work

Movement

Food & Water

Extra Notes and Observations

1 2 3 4 5   1 2 3 4 5   1 2 3 4 5

Weekly Intention and Notes

SUNDAY	MONDAY	TUESDAY	WEDNESDAY

Parts Work

Movement

Food & Water

| 1 2 3 4 5 | 1 2 3 4 5 | 1 2 3 4 5 | 1 2 3 4 5 |

SELF CARE THEME Some words that describe your Self care focus this week.

MONTH_____

THURSDAY	FRIDAY	SATURDAY
___	___	___

Parts Work

Movement

Food & Water

1 2 3 4 5   1 2 3 4 5   1 2 3 4 5

Extra Notes and Observations

Heart Centered Moments

What were your heart-centered moments like?
What makes you feel more present?

GLOWS, GROWS AND HIGHLIGHTS

_____
_____
_____
_____
_____
_____
_____
_____
_____
_____
_____
_____
_____
_____
_____
_____
_____
_____
_____
_____
_____
_____
_____
_____
_____
_____
_____
_____
_____

Endings and beginnings both share
reflection and hope.

ADAGE

$\mathcal{M}$onth

S	M	T	W	T	F	S

Weekly Intention and Notes

SUNDAY	MONDAY	TUESDAY	WEDNESDAY

Parts Work

Movement

Food & Water

1 2 3 4 5   1 2 3 4 5   1 2 3 4 5   1 2 3 4 5

SELF CARE THEME Some words that describe your Self care focus this week.

Month_____

THURSDAY _____

FRIDAY _____

SATURDAY _____

Extra Notes and Observations

Parts Work

Movement

Food & Water

1 2 3 4 5   1 2 3 4 5   1 2 3 4 5

Weekly Intention and Notes

SUNDAY	MONDAY	TUESDAY	WEDNESDAY

Parts Work

Movement

Food & Water

1 2 3 4 5   1 2 3 4 5   1 2 3 4 5   1 2 3 4 5

SELF CARE THEME Some words that describe your Self care focus this week.

MONTH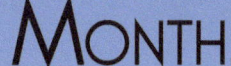_____

_____　　　　_____　　　　_____

Parts Work

_____　　_____　　_____
_____　　_____　　_____
_____　　_____　　_____
_____　　_____　　_____
_____　　_____　　_____
_____　　_____　　_____

Movement

_____　　_____　　_____
_____　　_____　　_____
_____　　_____　　_____
_____　　_____　　_____
_____　　_____　　_____

Food & Water

_____　　_____　　_____
_____　　_____　　_____
_____　　_____　　_____
_____　　_____　　_____
_____　　_____　　_____

1　2　3　4　5　　　1　2　3　4　5　　　1　2　3　4　5

WEEK-END REFLECTION PARTS WORK, NOTES GRATITUDE, HIGHLIGHTS

Extra Notes and Observations

Weekly Intention and Notes

SUNDAY	MONDAY	TUESDAY	WEDNESDAY

Parts Work

Movement

Food & Water

1 2 3 4 5   1 2 3 4 5   1 2 3 4 5   1 2 3 4 5

SELF CARE THEME Some words that describe your Self care focus this week.

MONTH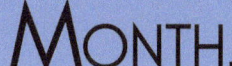_____

THURSDAY	FRIDAY	SATURDAY

Parts Work

Movement

Food & Water

1 2 3 4 5   1 2 3 4 5   1 2 3 4 5

Extra Notes and Observations

Weekly Intention and Notes

SUNDAY	MONDAY	TUESDAY	WEDNESDAY

Parts Work

Movement

Food & Water

1 2 3 4 5   1 2 3 4 5   1 2 3 4 5   1 2 3 4 5

SELF CARE THEME Some words that describe your Self care focus this week.

Month

THURSDAY	**FRIDAY**	**SATURDAY**

Extra Notes and Observations

Parts Work

Movement

Food & Water

1 2 3 4 5   1 2 3 4 5   1 2 3 4 5

Heart Centered Moments

What were your heart-centered moments like?
What makes you feel more present?

GLOWS, GROWS AND HIGHLIGHTS

Your body and inner parts are trying their best with what they have. Getting curious about their needs can be nourishing, healing, and empowering. Pace yourself with compassion.

HEART-CENTERED MOMENT PRACTICE

Month

S	M	T	W	T	F	S
☐	☐	☐	☐	☐	☐	☐
☐	☐	☐	☐	☐	☐	☐
☐	☐	☐	☐	☐	☐	☐
☐	☐	☐	☐	☐	☐	☐
☐	☐	☐	☐	☐	☐	☐
☐	☐	☐				

Weekly Intention and Notes

SUNDAY	MONDAY	TUESDAY	WEDNESDAY

Parts Work

Movement

Food & Water

1 2 3 4 5   1 2 3 4 5   1 2 3 4 5   1 2 3 4 5

SELF CARE THEME Some words that describe your Self care focus this week.

MONTH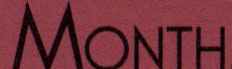

THURSDAY	**FRIDAY**	**SATURDAY**	**WEEK-END REFLECTION PARTS WORK, NOTES GRATITUDE, HIGHLIGHTS**

_____ _____ _____

Parts Work

Movement

Food & Water

Extra Notes and Observations

1 2 3 4 5   1 2 3 4 5   1 2 3 4 5

Weekly Intention and Notes

SUNDAY	MONDAY	TUESDAY	WEDNESDAY

Parts Work

Movement

Food & Water

1 2 3 4 5   1 2 3 4 5   1 2 3 4 5   1 2 3 4 5

SELF CARE THEME Some words that describe your Self care focus this week.

MONTH

THURSDAY _____

FRIDAY _____

SATURDAY _____

Parts Work

Movement

Food & Water

1 2 3 4 5   1 2 3 4 5   1 2 3 4 5

Weekly Intention and Notes

SUNDAY	MONDAY	TUESDAY	WEDNESDAY

Parts Work

Movement

Food & Water

| 1 2 3 4 5 | 1 2 3 4 5 | 1 2 3 4 5 | 1 2 3 4 5 |

SELF CARE THEME Some words that describe your Self care focus this week.

MONTH _____

	THURSDAY ____	**FRIDAY** ____	**SATURDAY** ____

Parts Work

Movement

Food & Water

1 2 3 4 5   1 2 3 4 5   1 2 3 4 5

WEEK-END REFLECTION PARTS WORK, NOTES GRATITUDE, HIGHLIGHTS

Extra Notes and Observations

Weekly Intention and Notes

SUNDAY	MONDAY	TUESDAY	WEDNESDAY

Parts Work

Movement

Food & Water

| 1 2 3 4 5 | 1 2 3 4 5 | 1 2 3 4 5 | 1 2 3 4 5 |

SELF CARE THEME Some words that describe your Self care focus this week.

MONTH_____

THURSDAY	FRIDAY	SATURDAY
____	____	____

Parts Work

Movement

Food & Water

1 2 3 4 5   1 2 3 4 5   1 2 3 4 5

Extra Notes and Observations

Heart Centered Moments

What were your heart-centered moments like?
What makes you feel more present?

GLOWS, GROWS AND HIGHLIGHTS

_____
_____
_____
_____
_____
_____
_____
_____
_____
_____
_____
_____
_____
_____
_____
_____
_____
_____
_____
_____
_____
_____
_____
_____
_____
_____
_____
_____
_____
_____

Many things in life may catch your eye, but only a few will capture your heart... pursue those.

ADAGE

Month

S	M	T	W	T	F	S
☐	☐	☐	☐	☐	☐	☐
☐	☐	☐	☐	☐	☐	☐
☐	☐	☐	☐	☐	☐	☐
☐	☐	☐	☐	☐	☐	☐
☐	☐	☐	☐	☐	☐	☐
☐	☐	☐				

Weekly Intention and Notes

SUNDAY	MONDAY	TUESDAY	WEDNESDAY

Parts Work

Movement

Food & Water

| 1 2 3 4 5 | 1 2 3 4 5 | 1 2 3 4 5 | 1 2 3 4 5 |

SELF CARE THEME Some words that describe your Self care focus this week.

Month 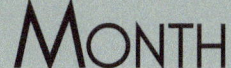 _____

THURSDAY	FRIDAY	SATURDAY
____	____	____

Parts Work

Movement

Food & Water

1 2 3 4 5   1 2 3 4 5   1 2 3 4 5

WEEK-END REFLECTION PARTS WORK, NOTES GRATITUDE, HIGHLIGHTS

Extra Notes and Observations

Weekly Intention and Notes

SUNDAY	MONDAY	TUESDAY	WEDNESDAY

Parts Work

Movement

Food & Water

| 1 2 3 4 5 | 1 2 3 4 5 | 1 2 3 4 5 | 1 2 3 4 5 |

SELF CARE THEME Some words that describe your Self care focus this week.

Month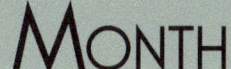_____

THURSDAY	**FRIDAY**	**SATURDAY**

_____   _____   _____

Parts Work

Movement

Food & Water

1 2 3 4 5   1 2 3 4 5   1 2 3 4 5

WEEK-END REFLECTION PARTS WORK, NOTES GRATITUDE, HIGHLIGHTS

Extra Notes and Observations

Weekly Intention and Notes

SUNDAY	MONDAY	TUESDAY	WEDNESDAY

Parts Work

Movement

Food & Water

1 2 3 4 5	1 2 3 4 5	1 2 3 4 5	1 2 3 4 5

SELF CARE THEME Some words that describe your Self care focus this week.

MONTH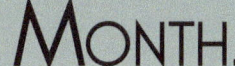

THURSDAY _____

FRIDAY _____

SATURDAY _____

Extra Notes and Observations

Parts Work

Movement

Food & Water

1 2 3 4 5   1 2 3 4 5   1 2 3 4 5

Weekly Intention and Notes

SUNDAY	MONDAY	TUESDAY	WEDNESDAY

Parts Work

Movement

Food & Water

| 1 2 3 4 5 | 1 2 3 4 5 | 1 2 3 4 5 | 1 2 3 4 5 |

SELF CARE THEME Some words that describe your Self care focus this week.

MONTH_____

THURSDAY	FRIDAY	SATURDAY

_____ _____ _____

Parts Work

Movement

Food & Water

1 2 3 4 5   1 2 3 4 5   1 2 3 4 5

Extra Notes and Observations

Heart Centered Moments

What were your heart-centered moments like?
What makes you feel more present?

GLOWS, GROWS AND HIGHLIGHTS

_____
_____
_____
_____
_____
_____
_____
_____
_____
_____
_____
_____
_____
_____
_____
_____
_____
_____
_____
_____
_____
_____
_____
_____

Happiness resides not in possessions, and not in gold. Happiness dwells in the soul.

DEMOCRITUS

Month

S	M	T	W	T	F	S
☐	☐	☐	☐	☐	☐	☐
☐	☐	☐	☐	☐	☐	☐
☐	☐	☐	☐	☐	☐	☐
☐	☐	☐	☐	☐	☐	☐
☐	☐	☐	☐	☐	☐	☐
☐	☐	☐				

Weekly Intention and Notes

SUNDAY	MONDAY	TUESDAY	WEDNESDAY

Parts Work

Movement

Food & Water

| 1 2 3 4 5 | 1 2 3 4 5 | 1 2 3 4 5 | 1 2 3 4 5 |

SELF CARE THEME Some words that describe your Self care focus this week.

MONTH

| THURSDAY | FRIDAY | SATURDAY | WEEK-END REFLECTION PARTS WORK, NOTES GRATITUDE, HIGHLIGHTS |

Parts Work

Movement

Food & Water

1 2 3 4 5   1 2 3 4 5   1 2 3 4 5

Extra Notes and Observations

Weekly Intention and Notes

SUNDAY	MONDAY	TUESDAY	WEDNESDAY

Parts Work

Movement

Food & Water

| 1 2 3 4 5 | 1 2 3 4 5 | 1 2 3 4 5 | 1 2 3 4 5 |

SELF CARE THEME Some words that describe your Self care focus this week.

MONTH_____

THURSDAY _____

FRIDAY _____

SATURDAY _____

Parts Work

Movement

Food & Water

1 2 3 4 5   1 2 3 4 5   1 2 3 4 5

Extra Notes and Observations

Weekly Intention and Notes

SUNDAY	MONDAY	TUESDAY	WEDNESDAY

Parts Work

Movement

Food & Water

1 2 3 4 5   1 2 3 4 5   1 2 3 4 5   1 2 3 4 5

SELF CARE THEME Some words that describe your Self care focus this week.

Month

THURSDAY	FRIDAY	SATURDAY

Parts Work

Movement

Food & Water

1 2 3 4 5   1 2 3 4 5   1 2 3 4 5

Extra Notes and Observations

Weekly Intention and Notes

SUNDAY	MONDAY	TUESDAY	WEDNESDAY

Parts Work

Movement

Food & Water

| 1 2 3 4 5 | 1 2 3 4 5 | 1 2 3 4 5 | 1 2 3 4 5 |

SELF CARE THEME Some words that describe your Self care focus this week.

Month_____

THURSDAY	FRIDAY	SATURDAY

_____ _____ _____

Parts Work

Movement

Food & Water

1 2 3 4 5   1 2 3 4 5   1 2 3 4 5

Extra Notes and Observations

Weekly Intention and Notes

	SUNDAY	MONDAY	TUESDAY	WEDNESDAY

Parts Work

Movement

Food & Water

1 2 3 4 5   1 2 3 4 5   1 2 3 4 5   1 2 3 4 5

SELF CARE THEME Some words that describe your Self care focus this week.

MONTH_____

THURSDAY _____

FRIDAY _____

SATURDAY _____

Parts Work

Movement

Food & Water

1 2 3 4 5   1 2 3 4 5   1 2 3 4 5

Extra Notes and Observations

Heart Centered Moments

What were your heart-centered moments like?
What makes you feel more present?

Glows, Grows and Highlights

_____
_____
_____
_____
_____
_____
_____
_____
_____
_____
_____
_____
_____
_____
_____
_____
_____
_____
_____
_____
_____
_____
_____
_____
_____

Feel the essence of connecting
with nature. Make it a habit.

HEART-CENTERED MOMENT PRACTICE

Month

S	M	T	W	T	F	S
☐	☐	☐	☐	☐	☐	☐
☐	☐	☐	☐	☐	☐	☐
☐	☐	☐	☐	☐	☐	☐
☐	☐	☐	☐	☐	☐	☐
☐	☐	☐	☐	☐	☐	☐
☐	☐	☐				

Weekly Intention and Notes

SUNDAY	MONDAY	TUESDAY	WEDNESDAY

Parts Work

Movement

Food & Water

1 2 3 4 5   1 2 3 4 5   1 2 3 4 5   1 2 3 4 5

SELF CARE THEME Some words that describe your Self care focus this week.

MONTH_____

THURSDAY	FRIDAY	SATURDAY

_____ _____ _____

Extra Notes and Observations

Parts Work

Movement

Food & Water

1 2 3 4 5   1 2 3 4 5   1 2 3 4 5

Weekly Intention and Notes

SUNDAY	MONDAY	TUESDAY	WEDNESDAY

Parts Work

Movement

Food & Water

1 2 3 4 5   1 2 3 4 5   1 2 3 4 5   1 2 3 4 5

SELF CARE THEME Some words that describe your Self care focus this week.

Month _____

THURSDAY _____ | **FRIDAY** _____ | **SATURDAY** _____

Parts Work

Movement

Food & Water

1 2 3 4 5   1 2 3 4 5   1 2 3 4 5

Extra Notes and Observations

Weekly Intention and Notes

SUNDAY	MONDAY	TUESDAY	WEDNESDAY

Parts Work

Movement

Food & Water

1 2 3 4 5   1 2 3 4 5   1 2 3 4 5   1 2 3 4 5

SELF CARE THEME Some words that describe your Self care focus this week.

Month

THURSDAY   _____

FRIDAY   _____

SATURDAY   _____

Parts Work

Movement

Food & Water

1 2 3 4 5   1 2 3 4 5   1 2 3 4 5

Extra Notes and Observations

Weekly Intention and Notes

SUNDAY	MONDAY	TUESDAY	WEDNESDAY

Parts Work

Movement

Food & Water

1 2 3 4 5   1 2 3 4 5   1 2 3 4 5   1 2 3 4 5

SELF CARE THEME Some words that describe your Self care focus this week.

MONTH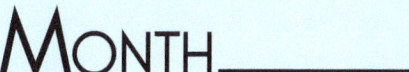_____

	THURSDAY	FRIDAY	SATURDAY
	_____	_____	_____

Parts Work

Movement

Food & Water

Thursday: 1 2 3 4 5

Friday: 1 2 3 4 5

Saturday: 1 2 3 4 5

Extra Notes and Observations

Heart Centered Moments

What were your heart-centered moments like?
What makes you feel more present?

GLOWS, GROWS AND HIGHLIGHTS

When you are inspired by some great purpose, some extraordinary project, all your thoughts break their bonds.

PATANJALI

Month

S	M	T	W	T	F	S

Weekly Intention and Notes

	SUNDAY	MONDAY	TUESDAY	WEDNESDAY
Parts Work	_____	_____	_____	_____
Movement				
Food & Water				
	1 2 3 4 5	1 2 3 4 5	1 2 3 4 5	1 2 3 4 5

SELF CARE THEME Some words that describe your Self care focus this week.

MONTH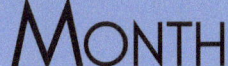_____

THURSDAY	FRIDAY	SATURDAY	WEEK-END REFLECTION PARTS WORK, NOTES GRATITUDE, HIGHLIGHTS

_____ _____   _____ _____   _____ _____

Extra Notes and Observations

Parts Work

Movement

Food & Water

1 2 3 4 5   1 2 3 4 5   1 2 3 4 5

Weekly Intention and Notes

SUNDAY	MONDAY	TUESDAY	WEDNESDAY

Parts Work

Movement

Food & Water

| 1 2 3 4 5 | 1 2 3 4 5 | 1 2 3 4 5 | 1 2 3 4 5 |

SELF CARE THEME Some words that describe your Self care focus this week.

Month 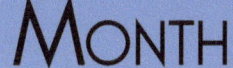_____

THURSDAY	FRIDAY	SATURDAY	WEEK-END REFLECTION PARTS WORK, NOTES GRATITUDE, HIGHLIGHTS

_____

Parts Work

Movement

Food & Water

1 2 3 4 5   1 2 3 4 5   1 2 3 4 5

Extra Notes and Observations

Weekly Intention and Notes

SUNDAY	MONDAY	TUESDAY	WEDNESDAY

Parts Work

Movement

Food & Water

1 2 3 4 5   1 2 3 4 5   1 2 3 4 5   1 2 3 4 5

SELF CARE THEME Some words that describe your Self care focus this week.

Month _____

THURSDAY	FRIDAY	SATURDAY
_____	_____	_____

Parts Work

Movement

Food & Water

1 2 3 4 5   1 2 3 4 5   1 2 3 4 5

Extra Notes and Observations

Weekly Intention and Notes

SUNDAY	MONDAY	TUESDAY	WEDNESDAY

Parts Work

Movement

Food & Water

1 2 3 4 5   1 2 3 4 5   1 2 3 4 5   1 2 3 4 5

SELF CARE THEME Some words that describe your Self care focus this week.

MONTH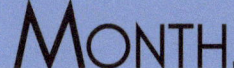_____

| | **THURSDAY** | **FRIDAY** | **SATURDAY** | **WEEK-END REFLECTION PARTS WORK, NOTES GRATITUDE, HIGHLIGHTS** |

_____

Extra Notes and Observations

Parts Work

_____
_____
_____
_____
_____

Movement

_____
_____
_____
_____
_____

Food & Water

_____
_____
_____
_____
_____

1 2 3 4 5   1 2 3 4 5   1 2 3 4 5

Heart Centered Moments

What were your heart-centered moments like?
What makes you feel more present?

GLOWS, GROWS AND HIGHLIGHTS

Love is like dew that falls on both
nettles and lilies.

SWEDISH PROVERB

Month

S   M   T   W   T   F   S

Weekly Intention and Notes

SUNDAY	MONDAY	TUESDAY	WEDNESDAY

Parts Work

Movement

Food & Water

SUNDAY	MONDAY	TUESDAY	WEDNESDAY
1 2 3 4 5	1 2 3 4 5	1 2 3 4 5	1 2 3 4 5

SELF CARE THEME Some words that describe your Self care focus this week.

MONTH_____

THURSDAY	FRIDAY	SATURDAY	WEEK-END REFLECTION PARTS WORK, NOTES GRATITUDE, HIGHLIGHTS

Parts Work

Movement

Food & Water

_____ _____ _____

Extra Notes and Observations

1 2 3 4 5   1 2 3 4 5   1 2 3 4 5

Weekly Intention and Notes

SUNDAY	MONDAY	TUESDAY	WEDNESDAY

Parts Work

Movement

Food & Water

1 2 3 4 5   1 2 3 4 5   1 2 3 4 5   1 2 3 4 5

SELF CARE THEME Some words that describe your Self care focus this week.

THURSDAY ___   **FRIDAY** ___   **SATURDAY** ___

WEEK-END REFLECTION PARTS WORK, NOTES GRATITUDE, HIGHLIGHTS

Extra Notes and Observations

Parts Work

_____

Movement

_____

Food & Water

_____

1 2 3 4 5   1 2 3 4 5   1 2 3 4 5

Weekly Intention and Notes

SUNDAY	MONDAY	TUESDAY	WEDNESDAY

Parts Work

Movement

Food & Water

| 1 2 3 4 5 | 1 2 3 4 5 | 1 2 3 4 5 | 1 2 3 4 5 |

SELF CARE THEME Some words that describe your Self care focus this week.

Month_____

THURSDAY	FRIDAY	SATURDAY
___ _____	___ _____	___ _____

Parts Work

Movement

Food & Water

| 1 2 3 4 5 | 1 2 3 4 5 | 1 2 3 4 5 |

Extra Notes and Observations

Weekly Intention and Notes

SUNDAY	MONDAY	TUESDAY	WEDNESDAY

Parts Work

Movement

Food & Water

SUNDAY	MONDAY	TUESDAY	WEDNESDAY
1 2 3 4 5	1 2 3 4 5	1 2 3 4 5	1 2 3 4 5

SELF CARE THEME Some words that describe your Self care focus this week.

MONTH

THURSDAY	FRIDAY	SATURDAY
_____	_____	_____

Parts Work

Movement

Food & Water

1 2 3 4 5   1 2 3 4 5   1 2 3 4 5

Extra Notes and Observations

Weekly Intention and Notes

SUNDAY	MONDAY	TUESDAY	WEDNESDAY

Parts Work

Movement

Food & Water

| 1 2 3 4 5 | 1 2 3 4 5 | 1 2 3 4 5 | 1 2 3 4 5 |

SELF CARE THEME Some words that describe your Self care focus this week.

Month_____

THURSDAY	FRIDAY	SATURDAY	WEEK-END REFLECTION PARTS WORK, NOTES GRATITUDE, HIGHLIGHTS

_____   _____   _____

Extra Notes and Observations

Parts Work

_____   _____   _____
_____   _____   _____
_____   _____   _____
_____   _____   _____

Movement

_____   _____   _____
_____   _____   _____
_____   _____   _____

Food & Water

_____   _____   _____
_____   _____   _____
_____   _____   _____

1 2 3 4 5   1 2 3 4 5   1 2 3 4 5

Heart Centered Moments

What were your heart-centered moments like?
What makes you feel more present?

GLOWS, GROWS AND HIGHLIGHTS

When the heart is at ease,
the body is healthy.

CHINESE PROVERB

Month

S	M	T	W	T	F	S

Weekly Intention and Notes

SUNDAY	MONDAY	TUESDAY	WEDNESDAY

Parts Work

Movement

Food & Water

| 1 2 3 4 5 | 1 2 3 4 5 | 1 2 3 4 5 | 1 2 3 4 5 |

SELF CARE THEME Some words that describe your Self care focus this week.

Month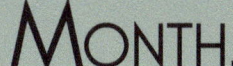_____

THURSDAY	FRIDAY	SATURDAY	WEEK-END REFLECTION PARTS WORK, NOTES GRATITUDE, HIGHLIGHTS

_____   _____   _____

Extra Notes and Observations

Parts Work

Movement

Food & Water

1 2 3 4 5   1 2 3 4 5   1 2 3 4 5

Weekly Intention and Notes

	SUNDAY	MONDAY	TUESDAY	WEDNESDAY

Parts Work

Movement

Food & Water

1 2 3 4 5   1 2 3 4 5   1 2 3 4 5   1 2 3 4 5

SELF CARE THEME Some words that describe your Self care focus this week.
_____
_____
_____
_____

Month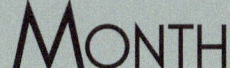

THURSDAY _____

FRIDAY _____

SATURDAY _____

Parts Work

Movement

Food & Water

1 2 3 4 5   1 2 3 4 5   1 2 3 4 5

Extra Notes and Observations

Weekly Intention and Notes

SUNDAY	MONDAY	TUESDAY	WEDNESDAY

Parts Work

_____

Movement

Food & Water

| 1 2 3 4 5 | 1 2 3 4 5 | 1 2 3 4 5 | 1 2 3 4 5 |

SELF CARE THEME Some words that describe your Self care focus this week.

MONTH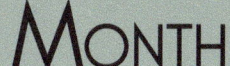_____

THURSDAY _____

FRIDAY _____

SATURDAY _____

Parts Work

Movement

Food & Water

1 2 3 4 5   1 2 3 4 5   1 2 3 4 5

Extra Notes and Observations

Weekly Intention and Notes

SUNDAY	MONDAY	TUESDAY	WEDNESDAY

Parts Work

Movement

Food & Water

| 1 2 3 4 5 | 1 2 3 4 5 | 1 2 3 4 5 | 1 2 3 4 5 |

SELF CARE THEME Some words that describe your Self care focus this week.

MONTH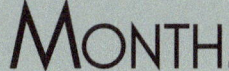

THURSDAY	FRIDAY	SATURDAY
————	————	————

Parts Work

Movement

Food & Water

1 2 3 4 5   1 2 3 4 5   1 2 3 4 5

Extra Notes and Observations

Heart Centered Moments

What were your heart-centered moments like?
What makes you feel more present?

GLOWS, GROWS AND HIGHLIGHTS

Eat to live, not live to eat.

SOCRATES

Month

S M T W T F S

Weekly Intention and Notes

SUNDAY	MONDAY	TUESDAY	WEDNESDAY

Parts Work

Movement

Food & Water

1 2 3 4 5   1 2 3 4 5   1 2 3 4 5   1 2 3 4 5

SELF CARE THEME Some words that describe your Self care focus this week.

MONTH _____

THURSDAY _____

FRIDAY _____

SATURDAY _____

Parts Work

_____
_____
_____
_____
_____
_____
_____

Movement

_____
_____
_____
_____
_____
_____

Food & Water

_____
_____
_____
_____
_____
_____

1 2 3 4 5   1 2 3 4 5   1 2 3 4 5

_____
_____
_____
_____
_____
_____

Extra Notes and Observations

_____
_____
_____
_____
_____
_____
_____
_____
_____
_____
_____
_____
_____
_____
_____
_____
_____
_____
_____
_____
_____
_____
_____
_____
_____
_____
_____

Weekly Intention and Notes

SUNDAY	MONDAY	TUESDAY	WEDNESDAY

Parts Work

Movement

Food & Water

SUNDAY: 1 2 3 4 5   MONDAY: 1 2 3 4 5   TUESDAY: 1 2 3 4 5   WEDNESDAY: 1 2 3 4 5

SELF CARE THEME Some words that describe your Self care focus this week.

MONTH _____

THURSDAY _____

FRIDAY _____

SATURDAY _____

Parts Work

_____
_____
_____
_____
_____
_____

Movement

_____
_____
_____
_____
_____
_____

Food & Water

_____
_____
_____
_____
_____
_____

1 2 3 4 5   1 2 3 4 5   1 2 3 4 5

_____
_____
_____
_____
_____

WEEK-END REFLECTION PARTS WORK, NOTES GRATITUDE, HIGHLIGHTS

Extra Notes and Observations

_____
_____
_____
_____
_____
_____
_____
_____
_____
_____
_____
_____
_____
_____
_____
_____
_____
_____
_____
_____
_____
_____
_____
_____
_____

Weekly Intention and Notes

SUNDAY	MONDAY	TUESDAY	WEDNESDAY

Parts Work

Movement

Food & Water

1 2 3 4 5	1 2 3 4 5	1 2 3 4 5	1 2 3 4 5

SELF CARE THEME Some words that describe your Self care focus this week.

Month_____

	THURSDAY	FRIDAY	SATURDAY

Parts Work

_____ _____ _____
_____ _____ _____
_____ _____ _____
_____ _____ _____
_____ _____ _____
_____ _____ _____

Movement

_____ _____ _____
_____ _____ _____
_____ _____ _____
_____ _____ _____
_____ _____ _____

Food & Water

_____ _____ _____
_____ _____ _____
_____ _____ _____
_____ _____ _____
_____ _____ _____

1 2 3 4 5 · 1 2 3 4 5 1 2 3 4 5

Extra Notes and Observations

Weekly Intention and Notes

SUNDAY	MONDAY	TUESDAY	WEDNESDAY

Parts Work

Movement

Food & Water

1 2 3 4 5   1 2 3 4 5   1 2 3 4 5   1 2 3 4 5

SELF CARE THEME Some words that describe your Self care focus this week.

MONTH

| THURSDAY | FRIDAY | SATURDAY | WEEK-END REFLECTION PARTS WORK, NOTES GRATITUDE, HIGHLIGHTS |

Parts Work

Movement

Food & Water

Extra Notes and Observations

1 2 3 4 5   1 2 3 4 5   1 2 3 4 5

Weekly Intention and Notes

SUNDAY	MONDAY	TUESDAY	WEDNESDAY

Parts Work

Movement

Food & Water

1 2 3 4 5   1 2 3 4 5   1 2 3 4 5   1 2 3 4 5

SELF CARE THEME Some words that describe your Self care focus this week.

MONTH

THURSDAY	FRIDAY	SATURDAY	WEEK-END REFLECTION PARTS WORK, NOTES GRATITUDE, HIGHLIGHTS

_____ _____ _____

Parts Work
_____
_____
_____
_____
_____
_____

Movement
_____
_____
_____
_____
_____

Food & Water
_____
_____
_____
_____
_____
_____

1 2 3 4 5   1 2 3 4 5   1 2 3 4 5

Extra Notes and Observations

Heart Centered Moments

What were your heart-centered moments like?
What makes you feel more present?

GLOWS, GROWS AND HIGHLIGHTS

A heartfelt compliment is a gift for both giver and recipient.

HEART-CENTERED MOMENT PRACTICE

Month

S	M	T	W	T	F	S

Weekly Intention and Notes

	SUNDAY	MONDAY	TUESDAY	WEDNESDAY
Parts Work				
Movement				
Food & Water				

1 2 3 4 5	1 2 3 4 5	1 2 3 4 5	1 2 3 4 5

SELF CARE THEME Some words that describe your Self care focus this week.

_____
_____
_____
_____
_____

MONTH

| | **THURSDAY** | **FRIDAY** | **SATURDAY** | **WEEK-END REFLECTION PARTS WORK, NOTES GRATITUDE, HIGHLIGHTS** |

Parts Work

Movement

Food & Water

1 2 3 4 5   1 2 3 4 5   1 2 3 4 5

Extra Notes and Observations

Weekly Intention and Notes

SUNDAY	MONDAY	TUESDAY	WEDNESDAY

Parts Work

Movement

Food & Water

1 2 3 4 5	1 2 3 4 5	1 2 3 4 5	1 2 3 4 5

SELF CARE THEME Some words that describe your Self care focus this week.

MONTH_____

THURSDAY

FRIDAY

SATURDAY

_____

Parts Work

Movement

Food & Water

1 2 3 4 5   1 2 3 4 5   1 2 3 4 5

Weekly Intention and Notes

SUNDAY	MONDAY	TUESDAY	WEDNESDAY

Parts Work

Movement

Food & Water

1 2 3 4 5   1 2 3 4 5   1 2 3 4 5   1 2 3 4 5

SELF CARE THEME Some words that describe your Self care focus this week.

MONTH_____

THURSDAY	FRIDAY	SATURDAY

_____ _____ _____

Parts Work

_____
_____
_____
_____
_____
_____
_____

Movement

_____
_____
_____
_____
_____
_____
_____
_____

Food & Water

_____
_____
_____
_____
_____
_____

1 2 3 4 5   1 2 3 4 5   1 2 3 4 5

WEEK-END REFLECTION PARTS
WORK, NOTES GRATITUDE,
HIGHLIGHTS

Extra Notes and Observations

Weekly Intention and Notes

SUNDAY	MONDAY	TUESDAY	WEDNESDAY

Parts Work

Movement

Food & Water

1 2 3 4 5	1 2 3 4 5	1 2 3 4 5	1 2 3 4 5

SELF CARE THEME Some words that describe your Self care focus this week.

Month _____

Thursday	**Friday**	**Saturday**	**Week-end reflection parts work, notes gratitude, highlights**

_____

Extra Notes and Observations

Parts Work

Movement

Food & Water

1 2 3 4 5   1 2 3 4 5   1 2 3 4 5

Heart Centered Moments

What were your heart-centered moments like?
What makes you feel more present?

GLOWS, GROWS AND HIGHLIGHTS

Imagine the color of calm.

HEART-CENTERED MOMENT PRACTICE

Month

S	M	T	W	T	F	S
☐	☐	☐	☐	☐	☐	☐
☐	☐	☐	☐	☐	☐	☐
☐	☐	☐	☐	☐	☐	☐
☐	☐	☐	☐	☐	☐	☐
☐	☐	☐	☐	☐	☐	☐
☐	☐	☐				

Weekly Intention and Notes

SUNDAY	MONDAY	TUESDAY	WEDNESDAY

Parts Work

_____ _____ _____ _____
_____ _____ _____ _____
_____ _____ _____ _____
_____ _____ _____ _____
_____ _____ _____ _____
_____ _____ _____ _____

Movement

_____ _____ _____ _____
_____ _____ _____ _____
_____ _____ _____ _____
_____ _____ _____ _____

Food & Water

_____ _____ _____ _____
_____ _____ _____ _____
_____ _____ _____ _____
_____ _____ _____ _____

1 2 3 4 5   1 2 3 4 5   1 2 3 4 5   1 2 3 4 5

SELF CARE THEME Some words that describe your Self care focus this week.

_____
_____
_____
_____

Month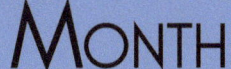

THURSDAY _____

FRIDAY _____

SATURDAY _____

Extra Notes and Observations

Parts Work

Movement

Food & Water

1 2 3 4 5   1 2 3 4 5   1 2 3 4 5

Weekly Intention and Notes

SUNDAY	MONDAY	TUESDAY	WEDNESDAY

Parts Work

Movement

Food & Water

1 2 3 4 5	1 2 3 4 5	1 2 3 4 5	1 2 3 4 5

SELF CARE THEME Some words that describe your Self care focus this week.

MONTH_____

THURSDAY	FRIDAY	SATURDAY
_____	_____	_____

Parts Work

Movement

Food & Water

Thursday: 1 2 3 4 5   Friday: 1 2 3 4 5   Saturday: 1 2 3 4 5

WEEK-END REFLECTION PARTS
WORK, NOTES GRATITUDE,
HIGHLIGHTS

Extra Notes and Observations

Weekly Intention and Notes

SUNDAY	MONDAY	TUESDAY	WEDNESDAY

Parts Work

Movement

Food & Water

1 2 3 4 5	1 2 3 4 5	1 2 3 4 5	1 2 3 4 5

SELF CARE THEME Some words that describe your Self care focus this week.

MONTH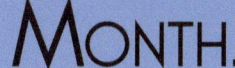_____

| THURSDAY | FRIDAY | SATURDAY | WEEK-END REFLECTION PARTS WORK, NOTES GRATITUDE, HIGHLIGHTS |

_____ _____

Extra Notes and Observations

Parts Work

Movement

Food & Water

1 2 3 4 5   1 2 3 4 5   1 2 3 4 5

Weekly Intention and Notes

SUNDAY	MONDAY	TUESDAY	WEDNESDAY

Parts Work

Movement

Food & Water

| 1 2 3 4 5 | 1 2 3 4 5 | 1 2 3 4 5 | 1 2 3 4 5 |

SELF CARE THEME Some words that describe your Self care focus this week.

Month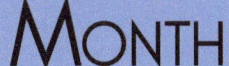_____

THURSDAY

FRIDAY

SATURDAY

Extra Notes and Observations

_____ _____ _____

Parts Work

Movement

Food & Water

1 2 3 4 5   1 2 3 4 5   1 2 3 4 5

Heart Centered Moments

What were your heart-centered moments like?
What makes you feel more present?

GLOWS, GROWS AND HIGHLIGHTS

Approach your inner journey with curiosity.

HEART-CENTERED MOMENT PRACTICE

Month

S	M	T	W	T	F	S

Weekly Intention and Notes

SUNDAY	MONDAY	TUESDAY	WEDNESDAY

Parts Work

Movement

Food & Water

1 2 3 4 5   1 2 3 4 5   1 2 3 4 5   1 2 3 4 5

SELF CARE THEME Some words that describe your Self care focus this week.

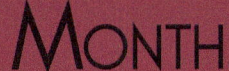

MONTH_____

THURSDAY

_____

_____
_____

Parts Work
_____
_____
_____
_____

Movement
_____
_____
_____
_____
_____

Food & Water
_____
_____
_____
_____
_____

1 2 3 4 5

FRIDAY

_____

_____
_____
_____
_____
_____
_____
_____
_____
_____
_____
_____
_____
_____
_____
_____

1 2 3 4 5

SATURDAY

_____

_____
_____
_____
_____
_____
_____
_____
_____
_____
_____
_____
_____
_____
_____
_____

1 2 3 4 5

**WEEK-END REFLECTION PARTS
WORK, NOTES GRATITUDE,
HIGHLIGHTS**

Extra Notes and Observations
_____
_____
_____
_____
_____
_____
_____
_____
_____
_____
_____
_____
_____
_____
_____
_____
_____
_____
_____
_____
_____
_____
_____
_____
_____
_____
_____
_____

_____
_____
_____
_____
_____

Weekly Intention and Notes

SUNDAY	MONDAY	TUESDAY	WEDNESDAY

Parts Work

Movement

Food & Water

1 2 3 4 5   1 2 3 4 5   1 2 3 4 5   1 2 3 4 5

SELF CARE THEME Some words that describe your Self care focus this week.

MONTH_____

THURSDAY	FRIDAY	SATURDAY

Extra Notes and Observations

Parts Work

_____ _____ _____

Movement

Food & Water

1 2 3 4 5   1 2 3 4 5   1 2 3 4 5

Weekly Intention and Notes

SUNDAY	MONDAY	TUESDAY	WEDNESDAY

Parts Work

Movement

Food & Water

SUNDAY	MONDAY	TUESDAY	WEDNESDAY
1 2 3 4 5	1 2 3 4 5	1 2 3 4 5	1 2 3 4 5

SELF CARE THEME Some words that describe your Self care focus this week.

MONTH _____

THURSDAY	FRIDAY	SATURDAY	WEEK-END REFLECTION PARTS WORK, NOTES GRATITUDE, HIGHLIGHTS

_____ _____ _____ Extra Notes and Observations

Parts Work

Movement

Food & Water

1 2 3 4 5   1 2 3 4 5   1 2 3 4 5

Weekly Intention and Notes

SUNDAY	MONDAY	TUESDAY	WEDNESDAY

Parts Work

Movement

Food & Water

| 1 2 3 4 5 | 1 2 3 4 5 | 1 2 3 4 5 | 1 2 3 4 5 |

SELF CARE THEME Some words that describe your Self care focus this week.

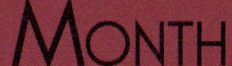

Month

THURSDAY	FRIDAY	SATURDAY

Parts Work

Movement

Food & Water

1 2 3 4 5   1 2 3 4 5   1 2 3 4 5

Extra Notes and Observations

Weekly Intention and Notes

SUNDAY	MONDAY	TUESDAY	WEDNESDAY

Parts Work

Movement

Food & Water

| 1 2 3 4 5 | 1 2 3 4 5 | 1 2 3 4 5 | 1 2 3 4 5 |

SELF CARE THEME Some words that describe your Self care focus this week.

Month _____

| THURSDAY | FRIDAY | SATURDAY | WEEK-END REFLECTION PARTS WORK, NOTES GRATITUDE, HIGHLIGHTS |

_____

Parts Work

Movement

Food & Water

1 2 3 4 5   1 2 3 4 5   1 2 3 4 5

Extra Notes and Observations

Heart Centered Moments

What were your heart-centered moments like?
What makes you feel more present?

GLOWS, GROWS AND HIGHLIGHTS

_____
_____
_____
_____
_____
_____
_____
_____
_____
_____
_____
_____
_____
_____
_____
_____
_____
_____
_____
_____
_____
_____
_____
_____
_____
_____
_____

If you do not change direction you
may end up where you are heading.

LAO TZU

Month

S	M	T	W	T	F	S

Weekly Intention and Notes

SUNDAY	MONDAY	TUESDAY	WEDNESDAY

Parts Work

Movement

Food & Water

1 2 3 4 5   1 2 3 4 5   1 2 3 4 5   1 2 3 4 5

SELF CARE THEME Some words that describe your Self care focus this week.

MONTH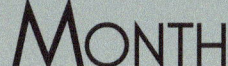

THURSDAY	FRIDAY	SATURDAY
_____	_____	_____

Parts Work

Movement

Food & Water

1 2 3 4 5   1 2 3 4 5   1 2 3 4 5

Extra Notes and Observations

Weekly Intention and Notes

SUNDAY	MONDAY	TUESDAY	WEDNESDAY

Parts Work

Movement

Food & Water

1 2 3 4 5   1 2 3 4 5   1 2 3 4 5   1 2 3 4 5

SELF CARE THEME Some words that describe your Self care focus this week.

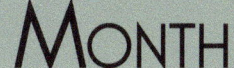

MONTH

| THURSDAY | FRIDAY | SATURDAY | WEEK-END REFLECTION PARTS WORK, NOTES GRATITUDE, HIGHLIGHTS |

Parts Work

Movement

Food & Water

Extra Notes and Observations

1 2 3 4 5   1 2 3 4 5   1 2 3 4 5

Weekly Intention and Notes

SUNDAY	MONDAY	TUESDAY	WEDNESDAY

Parts Work

Movement

Food & Water

1 2 3 4 5   1 2 3 4 5   1 2 3 4 5   1 2 3 4 5

SELF CARE THEME Some words that describe your Self care focus this week.

MONTH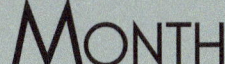_____

THURSDAY	FRIDAY	SATURDAY	WEEK-END REFLECTION PARTS WORK, NOTES GRATITUDE, HIGHLIGHTS

_____

Parts Work

_____
_____
_____
_____
_____
_____
_____
_____

Movement

_____
_____
_____
_____
_____
_____
_____

Food & Water

_____
_____
_____
_____
_____
_____
_____

1 2 3 4 5   1 2 3 4 5   1 2 3 4 5

Extra Notes and Observations

_____
_____
_____
_____
_____
_____
_____
_____
_____
_____
_____
_____
_____
_____
_____
_____
_____
_____
_____
_____
_____
_____
_____
_____
_____
_____
_____

Weekly Intention and Notes

SUNDAY	MONDAY	TUESDAY	WEDNESDAY

Parts Work

Movement

Food & Water

1 2 3 4 5   1 2 3 4 5   1 2 3 4 5   1 2 3 4 5

SELF CARE THEME Some words that describe your Self care focus this week.

MONTH_____

| THURSDAY | FRIDAY | SATURDAY | WEEK-END REFLECTION PARTS WORK, NOTES GRATITUDE, HIGHLIGHTS |

_____ _____ _____

Extra Notes and Observations

Parts Work

Movement

Food & Water

1 2 3 4 5   1 2 3 4 5   1 2 3 4 5

Heart Centered Moments

What were your heart-centered moments like?
What makes you feel more present?

GLOWS, GROWS AND HIGHLIGHTS

Theresa W. Velendzas MS is a Life & Wellness Coach who helps women struggling with self care. She is a Level 3 Certified IFS Practitioner and Personal Trainer & Corrective Exercise Specialist and is also trained in Mindfulness Based Stress Reduction (MBSR).

She holds degrees in Psychology and Health Care Management and is also inspired by her advocacy work to empower individualized optimal wellness. With insight from her own struggle with unusual weight gain and quest for sustainable self care, Theresa is passionate about helping others to live healthfully and joyfully.

Theresa's mission is to inspire ripples of care for self and others, one person at a time. A Greek-American living in Connecticut, Theresa, is mom to humans and various creatures. She loves vegetable gardening, road trips, and escaping to the beach whenever possible. Many of the featured pictures are her own.

Connect with her at Theresa@Altraform.com
or visit www.Altraform.com

Deborah Zafiropoulos is a multi-disciplinary creative with extensive experience in publishing. She holds an Industrial Design degree from Wentworth Institute of Technology in Boston, MA. Born on the west coast of the USA and raised in Europe, Deborah is currently freelancing from her home in Paris, France.

Connect with her at DZ9Designz@gmail.com

Acknowledgments

Motherhood has been my greatest inspiration for my own inward journey. M & P thank you. I am forever grateful for my wonderful teachers and mentors, including the privilege of studying with and being encouraged to explore this work by IFS founder Richard Schwartz Ph.D. Among all its valuable applications, IFS has been a catalyst in creating this mind-body blend for an evolution in wellness.

Heartfelt appreciation goes to my husband, parents, dear friends, mentors and colleagues for your curiosity, insightful questions, feedback, and devoted support. With special thanks to Shernett Edwards, Tammy Carlson, Anna Savvidou, Joanna Curry-Sartori, Arati Nair, and Jacqueline Germain. Your presence, thoughtful curiosity, and patience helped develop this with wider audiences in mind. Sincere gratitude to Brenda Sullivan of LivingAndLovinHerbs.com for her wonderful herbal recipes, wisdom, and support in materializing my vision.

Of course, none of this would have been possible without the beautiful designs and layouts by my beloved sister Deb. Onward!